LIFE *in* BRITAIN

—————— 1880-1919 ——————

LIFE *in* BRITAIN
1880-1919

N. HINDMARCH KEEN

Abbeydale Press

This paperback edition printed in 2009

© Copyright 1993 Bookmart Limited

ISBN: 978-1-86147-299-1

1 3 5 7 9 10 8 6 4 2

Published by Abbeydale Press,
an imprint of Bookmart Limited,
Registered Number 2372865
Trading as Bookmart Limited,
Blaby Road, Wigston,
Leicester, LE18 4SE, England

Printed in Thailand

CONTENTS

LIFE *in* BRITAIN

——— 1880-1919 ———

THE period between 1880 and 1919 saw some of the most dramatic changes in the entire history of Britain. It was during this time that the seeds of the modern way of life were sown. At the beginning of that period many of the things we now take for granted about our way of living simply did not exist. There were no cars on the roads, no aeroplanes in the sky, no television to relax with at the end of a working day, no pensions to look forward to at the end of a working life. Women had no right to vote at general elections and little chance of finding employment outside the home once they were married. Few ordinary working people could afford even such modest luxuries as a family holiday and for the majority of children working life began before they entered their teens.

By the end of the period all that had changed. The Britain of the Victorian era had been swept away by the onward march of technology and of new ideas – and by the terrible tide of war that had engulfed Europe in the summer of 1914.

THIS book is a photographic record of that period of change as it affected the everyday lives of the British people. Its pictures give us a glimpse of various ways of life, most of which have now gone for ever. What the camera has captured for us is what lies behind the history we read about in history books. The broad forces of that history are here, certainly. But they are reflected in the daily activities of the men, women and children who lived through them – in the eyes of society ladies strolling in the park and of ragged street-urchins sitting in the doorways of their houses in the slums, in the firm tread of the farmhand as he trudges behind his horse-drawn plough and the brisk step of the young men of Britain as they march off in their hundreds of thousands to the killing fields of France and Flanders. Men and women, rich and poor, young and old – people at work and at play, at home and at the sea-side, at peace and at war – these are the faces of a changing Britain that look out at us from the pages that follow.

Compared with the avalanche of change of the last 50 years, the developments that so astonished observers of the British way of life in the remarkable 40 years covered by this book may appear to us to have unfolded at a leisurely pace.

But the society in which they took place was itself a slower and more leisurely one than today's. In spite of all that had happened to change it since the Industrial Revolution began to make Britain the 'workshop of the world' in the late 18th century, the world of the 1880s would have been more recognisable to a time traveller from the reign of Queen Elizabeth I than the world of Queen Elizabeth II would be to a time traveller from the 1880s. Against this background, the great technological and social developments of the years around the turn of the century – developments that were to change the face of Britain for ever – stood out in stark and often frightening contrast.

So what was the country like as it stood on the threshold of these changes?

Britain in 1880 was the centre of an Empire that was still expanding rapidly and would soon take in a fifth of the world's land-mass and some 400 million of its people. Queen Victoria, now an ageing lady of 61, had been on the throne for 43 years. For the last four of those years she had counted among her various titles that of Empress of India, the land in which the majority of her subjects lived. A hugely popular monarch in her early years, Victoria had withdrawn from public life more and more since the death of her much-loved husband Prince Albert in 1861. There had for some time been mutterings of discontent about her withdrawn and distant style. But for all that, Queen Victoria was the only monarch most people could remember. She remained a sign of continuity in the face of change – the living representative of the great 'Victorian values' of family, duty and religion. The celebrations which were mounted throughout the country to mark the occasion of her Jubilee in 1887 were heartfelt and sincere.

Britain's far-flung Empire made her the foremost superpower of her time, but it also brought its problems. Little more than 20 years earlier, Britain's colonial rule in India had been bloodily challenged by a popular uprising that began in the ranks of the Bengal army and rapidly spread through the sub-continent. The Indian Mutiny was still a recent memory when, in 1880, Afrikaaners under the leadership of Paul Kruger rebelled against their British overlords in South Africa in the first of the two Boer wars, effectively winning independence for themselves in the Transvaal. The sun of Empire had not yet reached its highest point. The 'scramble for Africa' was only to begin over the next few years as the great colonial powers competed to extend and strengthen their territorial gains in the 'dark continent'. But there were already clouds on the horizon for the system of imperial rule.

THERE were strains in the social fabric of the nation too. Britain in 1880 was a land of contrasts – between town and country, rich and poor, employed and unemployed, men and women. The preceding century had seen a tidal wave of people flooding from the countryside into the towns in search of the employment opportunities offered by what we now call the Industrial Revolution. Settlements that were little more than villages at the beginning of the 19th century grew into major industrial towns teeming with thousands upon thousands of workers who had swapped the uncertain life of agriculture for jobs in the factory system. But while employment in the textile mills of Lancashire or the coal mines of Yorkshire or South Wales might not have been as insecure as work as an agricultural labourer, conditions were still appalling by modern standards, with long hours, low pay and dangerous working practices. By 1880 legislation had corrected some of the most flagrant abuses – for example, women and children under 10 years of age were no longer permitted to work underground in the coal industry – but there were plenty more for the fast-growing trade union movement to campaign against. Also, it would be more than 60 years before there was a system of universal welfare in Britain, and for the unemployed no work simply meant no income. Poverty remained widespread and it was not unusual to see starving children in the streets of Britain's major cities.

By the end of the 19th century the mass movement to the towns had left only one in five people living in the countryside in England and Wales – about the same number of people as lived in London. From being for the most part an agricultural society in the last years of the 18th century, Britain had become for the most part an urban one by the last years of the 19th. The deep agricultural depression caused by imports of cheap American grain from the 1870s onwards led even more people to leave the countryside in the years that followed. This is turn added to what were already appalling problems of overcrowding in the capital and other major towns, and the result was the further spread of the slums in which, all too often, disease and crime took a hold. Cholera, smallpox and diphtheria were common hazards of life in the 1880s. It was in that decade too that the term 'unemployment' first came to be used in its modern sense.

As the pictures in this book show, however, for many people at the beginning of the 1880s, Britain was by no means a gloomy place to live. Times were hard indeed for those who worked on the land and for those who had no work at all, but for most other people in the last decades of Queen Victoria's reign the standard of life was starting to improve. Wages were rising in real terms and families were becoming smaller than they had been earlier in the century. With more money in his pocket and fewer mouths to feed at home, the average working man began for the first time to find himself with a little extra cash left over after he had fed and clothed his family and paid the rent. Leisure was still in short supply, but more people were starting to find they could enjoy what little they had in ways – such as travelling for pleasure rather than out of sheer necessity – that had previously been available only to the well-to-do.

THERE were great contrasts in standard of living between those who had work and those who did not, and between those who lived in the country and those who had moved to the town. But they were as nothing compared with the contrast in standard of living between the rich and everyone else. In 1880 the vast majority of the country's wealth was still in the hands of a tiny minority of its people – the wealthy aristocracy and gentry. They also dominated the government, at both national and local level, and were largely responsible for the running of the Empire overseas. Theirs was the Britain of country houses and large estates, of hunting and shooting, and of the London 'season'. It was a world in which a young aristocrat like Frank Russell – the elder brother of the famous philosopher Bertrand Russell and grandson of the great reforming Prime Minister Lord John Russell – could drop in at the White House unannounced on a holiday visit to the United States and expect to be received by the President. This world had probably altered very little in the course of the preceding hundred

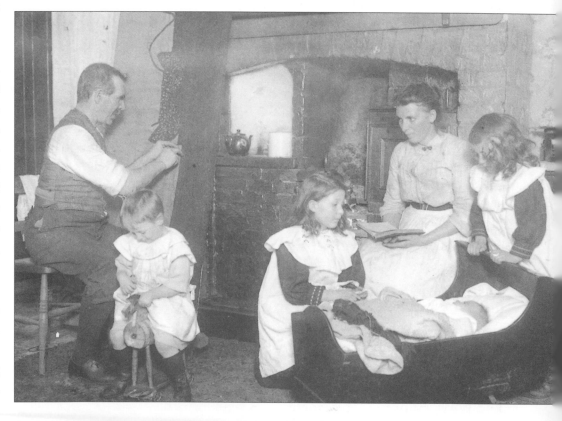

years, but here too things were changing. At the great public schools and universities, for example, the traditional training grounds of Britain's upper-class families, the sons of the aristocracy might, by the 1880s, find themselves rubbing shoulders with the sons of middle-class families who had achieved wealth and influence during the course of the 19th century.

Another notable contrast in Britain in 1880 was between the role of men and the role of women in society. Over the previous half-century, political reforms had given many more men the right to vote. Another Reform Act in 1887 would increase the electorate still further – though not to anything like its present size. But women were still excluded from voting (and would continue to be so until the end of the First World War) and not until 1882 could married women even own property in their own right. As for employment, most of the jobs that were open to unmarried women were as domestic servants – chambermaids, nurserymaids, kitchenmaids, and so on – while for married women, who were expected to stay at home and manage the household while their husbands went out to earn a living, there were virtually no jobs open at all.

This, then, was the state of the nation at the beginning of the period covered by this book. There had been changes, certainly, during the previous hundred years, but they were as nothing compared with the changes that were to come over the next hundred and which were already starting to make themselves felt as the 1880s got underway.

Perhaps the most far-reaching changes of the next four decades were those that occurred in the field of science and technology. Important as they were in themselves, many of these developments also were major factors in the broad social and economic changes that helped to shape the Britain of today. By the beginning of the 20th century, for example, the internal combustion engine was just starting to replace the horse in some of its roles as a source of power. The first motorised buses were taking over from the horse-drawn buses that had been the main form of public transport on Britain's roads for many years. Faster, cheaper and able to travel longer distances than horses, the new motor buses were to revolutionise people's travelling habits by bringing long journeys within reach of the average pocket. Many country folk could now travel outside their immediate neighbourhood for the first time. Day excursions, or trips to the coast for a summer holiday, were added to the ways in which ordinary people were able to spend their leisure time.

STILL more important for the future, though less significant in its effect on most people's lives at the time, was the appearance of the first motor cars in Britain. At the outset the new machines were expensive and unreliable. They were limited to a top speed of 20 miles per hour under legislation designed for steam traction engines. Within three years of the start of the 20th century, however, Henry Ford had set up his motor company in the United States in order to produce cheaper, more efficient cars in greater numbers. His Model T – affectionately known as the 'Tin Lizzie' – was launched a few years later. Ford's intention was to bring car ownership within the grasp of a wider public. The

Model T became a popular model in Britain for those who could afford it. From being the plaything of the wealthy few at the beginning of the century, the motor car was becoming a possibility for the many, and also a familiar, if not always welcome, sight on Britain's roads. It would be many years before Ford's dream of car ownership for the masses would become a reality, but a sign of the speed with which the new form of transport was catching on is the fact that 15 times more cars were licensed in Britain in 1913 than there had been a decade earlier.

The first decade of the 20th century saw another transport revolution too. In 1903, the very same year that the Ford Motor Company began trading in Detroit, two American engineers, the brothers Orville and Wilbur Wright, made the first successful flight in a heavier-than-air machine at Kittyhawk, North Carolina. Although the longest of the flights they managed on that December day lasted less than a minute and covered little more than 850 feet, theirs was an achievement of enormous significance for the future. Just as on roads and race tracks the new breed of motorists were already competing to set new speed records, so in the air others were soon vying to outdo the Wright Brothers' successes. In 1909 the French pilot Louis Blériot made the first cross-Channel flight – and earned himself a £1,000 prize from the *Daily Mail* in the process. However, as so often in the 20th century, it was war that gave the greatest stimulus to technological development. The Great War of 1914 to 1918 was the first in which air-power played a significant part. The aircraft that engaged the enemy in dog-fights over the trenches of the Western Front – bi-planes such as the Royal Flying Corps' Sopwith Camel – also pointed the way ahead for both military and civilian aviation.

A more modest transport revolution, but one that had a more immediate effect on the lives of ordinary people, came with Dunlop's development of the pneumatic tyre in the 1880s. One of its first uses was on the bicycle. Until then, cycling had been a somewhat uncomfortable affair – it was not for nothing that the early bicycles were known as 'bone-shakers'! – but the introduction of the new pneumatic-tyred 'safety bicycle' opened up the joys and conveniences of cycling to many more people. Cycling became a craze from the 1880s onwards, with men and women alike taking to the saddle of a bike. Not long before they could only have taken to the saddle of a horse, or to 'Shanks' pony'.

Another milestone on the road towards the age of mass communications in which we now live was passed in 1901 when the Italian physicist Marconi sent the first transatlantic wireless message. The potential of the new medium was dramatically shown nine years later when the notorious wife-murderer Dr Crippen was arrested on board ship as he tried to flee the country with his young lover, who was disguised as a boy. The captain of the ship on which they were travelling became suspicious of the two passengers and radioed the mainland, from where a police officer sailed out to arrest Crippen at sea. Much publicised at the time, the part played by wireless in the case – the first criminal investigation to be concluded by such means – caught the imagination of the British public, but it would be some years before a wireless set became a common feature in homes around the country.

THE early years of the new century also saw such new applications of technology as the electric light, the telephone and the gramophone – all of which dated from the last decades of Queen Victoria's reign – finding their way into the homes of the well-to-do. The first silent film had been shown in London in 1896. The same year saw the launch of Britain's first mass-market daily newspaper, the *Daily Mail*. The world's first purpose-built cinema opened in the Lancashire town of Colne in 1907. The music hall remained one of the most popular forms of entertainment outside the home, but today's mass-media society was already struggling to be born.

In the world of politics too the period from 1880 to 1919 saw far-reaching changes. The long Victorian era came to a formal end in 1901 with the death of the old Queen at the grand old age of 81. Her state funeral was an occasion of great national mourning. The fact that it was captured on moving film – the footage can still be seen today – was in itself a sign of how far the world had changed since her accession to the throne 63 years earlier. In 1898 and 1903 two of the towering figures of the Victorian political scene, the former Prime Ministers William Ewart Gladstone and Lord Salisbury, also died. The three deaths give a sense of an end of an era in the life of the nation.

The new King, Edward VII, was 59 years old and had always lived a life that was in stark contrast to that of his puritanical mother. Indeed, Victoria had so disapproved of her son's pleasure-loving ways that she had virtually excluded him from any political role while she was alive. But this did not stop him being immensely popular, both as Prince of Wales and as King, with the mass of the British public as well as with the glittering aristocratic social circle of which he was the centre. Related by blood or marriage to many of the other crowned heads of Europe – the German Kaiser Wilhelm II was his nephew and the Russian Tsar Nicholas II his niece's husband – Edward VII was a major figure on the international stage and gained the reputation of being a peace-maker. His state visits overseas, often in fact royal family get-togethers, were much reported at home. His short reign ended with his death from pneumonia in 1910. His son, the grandfather of the present Queen, succeeded him as King George V.

ALTHOUGH Edward VII's reign is often thought of as a 'golden summer', a last time of stability before the old certainties of British life were swept away on the tide of the First World War, the forces of political change were already at work. The last decades of Queen Victoria's reign had seen the same alternation of Tory and Liberal governments as in much of the 19th century, though the big issue of the 1880s and 1890s was no longer free trade, as it had been earlier in the century, but the vexed question of Irish Home Rule. The new century, however, also saw a new political force emerge onto the national stage.

The Labour Representation Committee, which changed its name to the Labour Party in 1909, was created in 1900. Its leaders were the former coal-miner Keir Hardie and the future Prime Minister Ramsay MacDonald. Its aims were to secure greater representation in Parliament for the average working man. The birth of the new party was an unmistakable sign of the times. For some years organised labour had been campaigning for better conditions and a stronger political voice. Such victories as the Bryant & May match girls' strike of 1888 and the London dock strike of the following year had encouraged the growth of a new and more organised form of trade unionism. In the first years of the 20th century the number of people joining trade unions, many of which were now affiliated to the new Labour Party, increased dramatically. In the 12 years after 1901 trade union membership in Britain more than doubled to above 4 million. Large-scale strikes in the rail, coal and dock industries won better pay and conditions for many workers.

ONE group that initially benefited less than most from these changes comprised a very large part of the nation: the female population of Great Britain. But that too was about to change. At the start of the period covered by this book women were not allowed to vote in national elections. In fact married women were not even permitted to own property in their own right. Most women who had jobs outside the home were domestic servants. In those jobs, although physical conditions were often a distinct improvement on what they might have experienced had they remained at home, there was little protection against harsh employers.

However, a service sector had grown up during

Victorian times, supplying industry and those who worked in it with everything from banking and insurance services to groceries. These new shops and offices not only offered clerical and counter jobs to young men who might in earlier years have gone to work in the factories, but also provided new employment opportunities for women as typists, clerks and shop assistants. The great break came, however, with the outbreak of the First World War in August 1914. Multitudes of young men volunteered for the front immediately, and later, when the flood of volunteers slowed to a trickle, conscription robbed the country's commerce and industry of yet more of its male labour force. This left vacancies in offices, shops and factories throughout the land, and women were quick to step into the breach. Women also played a more direct and equally vital part in the war effort by working in munitions factories at home and by caring for the wounded by nursing at the front. There they showed qualities of dedication, courage and efficiency previously unsuspected by many of their menfolk. When the hostilities ended in 1918 many women were forced to return to their traditional roles, but the first step had been taken. The ultimate goal was equal employment opportunities with men, and further steps towards that would be taken during and after the Second World War a quarter of a century later.

Meanwhile, women had also been campaigning for a political voice of their own. The question of votes for women had been on the agenda ever since the electoral reforms of 1867. It was only in the last two decades of the 19th century that the campaign for woman's suffrage really went into top gear. Various different groups were formed, with various different approaches to the matter. They met with little success in their attempts to persuade an overwhelmingly male establishment to agree to what they wanted. It was this failure which led to the emergence in 1903 of a more militant wing of the suffrage movement with the formation of the Women's Political and Social Union (WPSU) under the able leadership of Mrs Emmeline Pankhurst.

The WPSU, whose members were soon to be dubbed 'suffragettes', increasingly pursued a campaign of direct action to achieve their ends. This included demonstrations and attacks on property and, in some cases, on policemen and politicians. That alienated many potential supporters but also gave the cause a much higher profile than it had had before. Events such as the death of Emily Davison – she was killed under the hooves of the King's horse when she tried to grab its reins during the 1913 Derby – were widely reported. So too were various bomb attacks on the houses of leading establishment figures, including that of the then Chancellor of the Exchequer, David Lloyd George. Such acts led to the imprisonment of many suffragettes, including Mrs Pankhurst herself. Some went on hunger-strike and were force-fed by doctors and warders. This move caused widespread outrage. It was followed by the so-called 'Cat and Mouse' Act of 1913,

under which hunger-striking women could be released from prison, only to be rearrested later.

Despite all these efforts, however, it was not until after the First World War – during which many of the campaigners, including Mrs Pankhurst, threw their weight behind the government's recruitment drives – that women were able to vote in a general election. Even then the right was limited to women over the age of 30 who were ratepayers or the wives of ratepayers.

The years 1880 to 1919 saw numerous other changes to the social fabric of Britain. In 1880 elementary education had become compulsory for the first time in Britain. Not until 1891 was elementary education made free, and it was 1893 before the school leaving age was raised to 11. Secondary education was restructured around the turn of the century, and such services as free school meals and medical inspections were introduced in the years running up to the First World War. By 1918, in a major advance on the position only a few years earlier, all children between the ages of 5 and 14 were required by law to go to school. Britain was becoming a better-educated country.

It was becoming a healthier country too, and one in which people were better provided for in their old age and in times of need. For it was during the four decades covered by *Faces of Britain* that the Poor Laws, under which financial relief for the needy had been handed out for centuries, were finally replaced by a more modern system of state welfare provision. For the first time this included old age pensions and contributions to a national insurance scheme from which unemployment and sickness benefits could be paid.

ALL these changes – scientific and technological, social and political – left their mark on the face of Britain, as the photographs in this book show. But perhaps nothing changed it as deeply and finally as the momentous events that were unfolding on the international stage as we enter the last decade of our story – the decade that was to end with the horror of the First World War.

Britain's overseas Empire had expanded enormously since 1880, particularly in Africa. That expansion was partly the result of a search for new markets in the face of much stronger economic competition from the growing power of the United States and of Germany. What is more, the second Boer War – which broke out in 1899 and proved a longer, uglier and vastly more expensive affair than the first one – had made Britain's political leaders take a long, hard look at their foreign policy. What they saw was their own international isolation and the threat posed to Britannia's mastery of the waves by the rapid growth of the German navy. Their response was to set up informal alliances with France and Russia.

It was against this background that the tensions which erupted into war in August 1914 played themselves out. The shot that killed the Archduke Franz Ferdinand in Sarajevo set in motion an unstoppable train of events. The great powers – Austria and Germany

on the one hand and France, Russia and Britain on the other – rapidly mobilised for war. When the Kaiser's forces invaded Belgium, whose neutrality Britain had sworn to defend, Britain's involvement in that war became inevitable. Within weeks what had begun as a patriotic crusade degenerated into the nightmare of mud and slaughter that was the Western Front. As the military strategies of the 19th century met the machine-guns of the 20th, the war that was to have been over by Christmas dragged on for four dark years.

The human cost of the war was appallingly high. Britain alone lost three-quarters of a million dead, and there was hardly a home untouched by the tragedy. For those who came back, life would never be the same again. The Britain they returned to was a very different place from the one their parents and grandparents had known in 1880. The challenges before it were those of a modern age, but so were many of the tools with which it faced them. Many new changes lay ahead, changes that would have been unthinkable only 40 years earlier. But it was those that had already taken place – those of the decades whose faces are recorded in this book – that laid the foundations of the Britain we know today.

THE COST OF LIVING AROUND THE 1880s AND THE 1890s

Commodities

Jordan's almonds	10p per lb
Garibaldi biscuits	1½p per lb
Golden syrup/treacle	5p for 7lb
Lard	2½p per lb
Bread (in 1915)	3½p for 4lb
Butter (1915–20)	13p per lb
Beer (1918)	2½p per pint
Safety matches	3½p per dozen boxes
Cigars	1p each
Fountain pen	32½p
Football	35p
Man's trousers	37p
Man's shirt	6½p

Transport

Bus fare (Paddington to Mansion House 1915–20)	4d (nearly 2p)
Rail fare (London to Manchester – 189 miles – in 1928)	£1.18p

SCHOOL LEAVING AGE

1893	11 years
1899	12 years

INCOMES

1890–1914

Agricultural labourer	90p per week
Butler	£100 per annum
Footman (upper)	£50 per annum
Cook/Housekeeper	£80 per annum
Governess	£75 per annum
Head housemaid	£30 per annum
Miner	£1.75 per week
Nanny	£40 per annum
Skilled worker (general)	£1.90 per week
Clerk (railway)	£1.50 per week
Foreman (general)	£2.25 per week
Clerk (bank)	£2.80 per week
Clerk (civil service)	£116 per annum
Clerk (business)	£96 per annum
Bricklayer	£2.06 per week
Manager	£250 per annum
Village schoolmaster	£200 per annum

AVERAGE WEEKLY HOURS OF WORK LONDON, 1880–1914

Engineering	52 hours
Printing Industry	53 hours
Furniture Manufacture (cabinet maker)	52 hours

CITY LIFE

IN the Victorian era massive migration of people from the British countryside into the cities continued. It had begun with the Industrial Revolution at the end of the 18th century. By the time Queen Victoria died in 1901 only one-fifth of the people of England and Wales still lived in the countryside. In the 60 years after the Great Exhibition of 1851, London more than tripled in size, and the capital had 7.3 million inhabitants by 1911 – not far short of a fifth of the entire population of mainland Britain.

This huge influx of people brought new problems, but it also brought new opportunities. The rapid growth of population in the towns led in many areas to chronic overcrowding. It also led to a sprawl of new suburbs that were often unplanned and breeding-grounds for disease and crime. But it also brought with it a new vitality. Increases in the power of local government helped to foster a new sense of community, especially in the large industrial towns of the Midlands and the North of England. A sense of civic pride can be seen in the grand municipal buildings that began to appear in town centres in the last decades of the 19th century. These buildings – town halls, public libraries, art galleries, museums and concert halls – are often among the most impressive examples of Victorian architecture. They are symbols of the cultural liveliness and spirit of self-improvement that were features of life in the late Victorian and early 20th-century city.

A new pattern of urban life developed along with all these changes. In the major cities such as London, Birmingham and Manchester people began to commute from the ever-spreading suburbs by train or bus. The daily movement of workers created traffic problems we have still not solved today. The everyday life of many junior and middle-ranking professionals belonging to the new suburbs was one of some comfort, and one in which decency and respectability were the standards of almost everyone.

LONDON in the rain. Passengers, wisely confining themselves to the inside of an open-top bus, find their journey delayed as a policeman holds up traffic in Westminster to allow Members of Parliament to cross to the House of Commons.

A S British cities became ever more crowded during the 19th century, town planners recognised the need to preserve open spaces. In towns and cities throughout the country, urban parks offered an escape from the noise and bustle of the surrounding streets. The great parks of central London had been a feature of life in the capital for centuries. Many of them were originally royal preserves, to which the public had been allowed access. Gradually they became part of the city that grew up around them. Hyde Park, once a royal deer park, had been a fashionable place to see and be seen ever since Charles I opened it to the public in the middle of the 17th century. As can be seen from these pictures of upper-class ladies taking their dogs for a stroll there in 1912, this tradition was still very much alive in the years leading up to the First World War.

LUNCHTIME in the City: Edwardian professionals in bowlers and boaters enjoy the midday sunshine in London's Temple Gardens. For some, lunchtime concerts like these were a chance to relax and listen to the music of the band. Others obviously preferred to catch up with the papers, then full of news about the new Prime Minister, Herbert Henry Asquith. He had come to power only a few weeks before this photograph was taken in June 1908.

CHILDREN will always find games to play and mischief to get up to, but the grim conditions of life in the city slums of late 19th- and early 20th-century Britain must have subdued even the most carefree street urchin. The two little boys and the girl photographed at their street door in August 1910 *(opposite bottom)* look old and exhausted beyond their years. Children were often hungry and ill as a result of the poverty-stricken and unhealthy conditions in which

they lived. It is easy to see how children like these might have been tempted into crime. The urge may have been to obtain things their families could not afford – or perhaps simply to eat.

The health of the country's young people was a matter of urgent concern at about the time these photographs were taken. A government report in 1906 found evidence of serious malnutrition and made arrangements for local authorities to provide

meals for children in need. In the picture above, East End children, waving their admission tickets, gather outside the Brunswick Hall in London's Whitechapel to claim halfpenny Christmas dinners: they cost a halfpenny each. Cities in the provinces were not without their problems of childhood poverty, as can be seen from this picture of two ragged boys about to receive new suits from the Plymouth police clothing fund for the poor.

HEAVY traffic is not simply a late 20th-century problem, as these photographs of Victorian London show. In the days before motorised transport, the graceful crescents of Regent Street *(above)* would have echoed to the constant sound of horses' hooves and tyreless wheels. Traffic congestion was a familiar sight in Ludgate Hill even in 1890 *(left)*. No doubt the passengers in the steam train seen crossing the bridge here congratulated themselves on opting to travel by rail!

HORSE-POWER ON THE STREET

THE staggering growth in the population of many of Britain's cities in the Victorian period resulted in the first appearance of one of the problems of the modern age: traffic jams. Before this period, most people lived very close to where they earned their living. From now on, many needed to get to and from work, and in London a network of commuter railway lines brought passengers in from the suburbs in huge numbers every day. Nowadays we look back on the heyday of steam trains with nostalgia. We forget how noisy, dirty and unhealthy they were – especially on the underground system. That seemed a revolutionary development in its day, but it was served by steam engines, like the overground railway.

It is easy to have a false impression of the buses and cabs shown on this page as well. They were certainly more graceful in design than the ones we see on the roads

today. However, the horse-drawn transport which used the country's roads until the introduction of the motorbus in the early years of the 20th century was incredibly noisy. Further, the pollution that it brought was of an even smellier kind than petrol and diesel fumes! In fact, when the horse began to give way to the internal combustion engine, most city-dwellers noticed that their towns became quieter and cleaner.

Motor taxis began to appear on the streets of London in the first decade of the 20th century, drivers of horse-drawn hansom cabs such as the one shown here *(above left)* were furious, and at least some of the breakdowns that plagued the new taxis were the result of sabotage. Perhaps putting a zebra between the shafts *(bottom right)* was a last-ditch attempt to hold on to customers by sheer force of novelty!

LEFT: Polling stations in towns throughout the country had their first sight of women voting in a general election in 1918. This peaceful scene is of nurses casting their votes in the so-called 'coupon election' of December that year. It gives little hint of the long and often bitter struggle of the suffragettes which had enabled them to do so. Sweeping changes had taken place in the electoral system in 1918, when the Representation of the People Act tripled the number of people eligible to vote in Britain. The 21 million Britons who had the right to go to the polls now included women for the first time – but only women over 30 who were ratepayers or the wives of ratepayers.

BELOW: Election fun for all the family. The children of the local candidate rally to their father's cause in Hastings in 1908.

ABOVE: Electioneering was a community affair in the early years of the 20th century. In this photograph, taken during a by-election in Bethnal Green in the East End of London in 1914, the voters of the future throw their weight behind the candidate of today. Without the benefit of television and radio broadcasts, candidates' chances of success depended on their being able to meet as many of their constituents as they could, and to persuade them to support them on the big day.

COUNTRY LIFE

THE British countryside in the years around the turn of the century looked much the same as it had over the previous three hundred years. But the traditional way of life of those who lived outside towns was starting to disappear. One reason was that many people had left the countryside during the last quarter of the 19th century when imports of cheap American wheat forced British grain prices downwards and plunged the country into a deep agricultural depression. At the same time, the first experiments in farm mechanisation were beginning to change patterns of working life that went back to before the Middle Ages. Among the earliest of the steps towards modernity was the introduction of the steam-driven threshing machine in the 1860s. Developments such as this were the first stirrings of a revolution that would sweep the long-established rural world away for ever.

At the same time improvements in roads and methods of transport were opening up the countryside in ways undreamt of a generation earlier. For centuries the boundary of the parish had also been the boundary of the lives of most of the people who lived in it. Even the coming of the railways, which linked the major towns together but left most villages untouched, had done little to change this. However, the early years of the 20th century saw the development of cheap motorised bus services. The result was that longer and more regular journeys came within the reach of the average country person for the first time.

With the opening up of the world outside their own villages came a number of new influences on the country-dweller. There were political changes in the nation at large, such as increases in the numbers of those eligible to vote and great improvements in education. Alongside these came the first strains in the social structure. In the countryside in particular the pattern of local aristocracy, gentry and working folk had survived intact for generations. The most powerful impact on it at this time was the outbreak of hostilities. The young men who marched off to the First World War from villages across the country in August 1914 would fight shoulder to shoulder with comrades from all social classes.

COUNTING sheep: Local farmers prepare to make their bids to the auctioneer at the Truro fatstock show shortly after the end of the First World War.

OPPOSITE top: Until large-scale mechanisation began, after the Second World War, farming methods in Britain had changed little for centuries. The clothes would have looked unfamiliar, but the medieval ploughman would have recognised his 1920 successor, seen here with a pair of magnificent chestnuts.

OPPOSITE bottom: Haymaking near Ambleside in 1910. Haymaking and gleaning were still important events in the country calendar at the turn of the century. Each involved entire communities in days of wearisome toil in the fields. In early summer, men, women and children would all join in forking up the hay and carting it off to haystacks for storage. With the harvest safely gathered in, the gleanings of grain left behind by the reapers were a welcome free bonus for cottagers.

ABOVE: An early experiment in mechanisation. A farmer is seen here mounting a 'patent land digger' on the side of his steam tractor in 1902. Most farmers at this time, however, continued to rely on horsepower.

COUNTRY CHARACTERS

THE countryside was a place of many callings. The often colourful characters who pursued them were part of the fabric of rural life in Britain. Many of the country trades and skills that survived from Victorian times into the 20th century have now disappeared for ever, and the tools and implements that were used – which had sometimes been features of the village scene for generations – can now be seen only in museums.

The mower returning from the fields with his long-handled scythe and his earthenware flagon of cider *(top left)* was a familiar sight at harvest-time in the days before the combine harvester. It was not just the gathering in of the crops that relied on the sheer physical strength of countrymen and women. The whole of the farm cycle depended on back-breaking individual labour. Compare, for example, the work of the ploughman guiding his plough across muddy, stony fields behind a team of oxen or horses *(opposite bottom)* with that required of the modern tractor-driver.

Some occupations, such as sheep-shearing, here seen taking place in Ambleside in 1910 *(opposite top)*, continue with very little change to this day. But many more were part of a vanished era. There were the blacksmiths, whose forges provided shoes for the horses that were the main source of power in Britain's rural communities. There were the charcoal-burners, whose turf- or heather-roofed huts were a familiar feature of woods and forests. The carters and wheelwrights, the mole-catchers and warreners, and even the itinerant pedlars, provided services that kept the wheels of village life turning. All these now belong, like these Devon shepherds *(opposite middle)* and this Victorian country family eating a rough meal of bread and soup at their cottage door *(bottom left)*, to the past.

ABOVE: The end of the day's toil. A cottager leans on his gate to watch the world go by. The farm worker was the backbone of the rural economy. The introduction of intensive farming methods in the second half of the 20th century saw many of his traditional tasks taken over by the machine. Although he fed the mouths of the nation, long and irregular hours and low wages meant that his own life was often a hard and hungry one.

RIGHT: The way of life of the Scottish crofter was one of the hardest in Britain's rural communities. As can be seen from this photograph, taken in the Shetland Islands in about 1900, living conditions were often primitive and comforts few and far between. In order to make ends meet, the crofter and his family turned their hand to many tasks, from tilling and grazing to fishing and weaving.

ABOVE: The workers at a Norfolk turkey farm pose for the camera in March 1906, complete with examples of their stock-in-trade at different stages of the production process. The two boys in the centre of the picture are holding live birds; others have already been killed and plucked. During the course of the 19th century the turkey had taken over from the goose as the favoured Christmas bird and Norfolk turkeys were particularly prized.

OPPOSITE top: Milking time. Milkmaids demonstrate their skills at an agricultural show in 1912. At the turn of the century, milking was often done in the fields, with milkmaids like these taking their pails out to the cows rather than bringing the cows in to the milking sheds as is the practice today. It is unlikely, however, that they would have turned out in such immaculate white frocks and 'petal' hats if they had been at home on the farm.

LEFT: A French expert gives two lady market gardeners the benefit of his experience in continental methods on a visit to a fruit and vegetable farm at Thatcham, near Newbury in Berkshire. This photograph, which shows crops being grown under bell-shaped cloches in the background, was taken in March 1908.

WORKING LIFE

THE years from 1880 to 1920 were on the whole a good time to be in work in Britain – except for those trying to make a living in farming. In the closing years of the Victorian age real wages rose. Working people found for the first time that they had both leisure time and spare money with which to enjoy it. Encouraged by such victories as a strike by match-girls at the Bryant & May factory, trade unionism gathered strength. The result was better conditions in many areas of working life. New legislation shortened working hours and restricted the use of child labour.

Patterns of employment were changing too. Men who had made their fortune in manufacturing now commonly sent their sons not into the family business but to public schools. If possible, they went on to university in order to enter a professional career in medicine, the law, the Church or the civil service. A new service sector had grown up alongside the manufacturing industries, offering new opportunities for bright young men in banking, insurance, accounting and retailing. At the beginning of the 19th century Napoleon had described Britain as a nation of shop-keepers; now she was becoming a nation of book-keepers too. In addition, the expansion of the cities meant that there was a new demand for skilled workers to plumb, wire and fit out the suburban homes of the rising middle classes.

This was also the time when women began to find their way into different types of work outside the home. Previously, the only jobs for them were in domestic service. But as their menfolk went off to war in 1914, women rose to the challenge of filling the jobs they left vacant. They proved themselves every bit as capable as their husbands, sons and brothers. It was not to last. When the war was over, many women were forced to go back to domestic work. But many of the soldiers returning from the front also found themselves with no paid work to do. The word 'unemployment' was first used in the 1880s; by the beginning of the 1920s more and more people were coming to know its meaning. For the unlucky ones during this period there was no working life at all.

⁘

THE sweat of their brows. Workmen, proving that roadworks are nothing new, break for a well-earned mug of tea and a chat.

OPPOSITE top: The hard life of Britain's coalminers at the turn of the century was not without its lighter side. The community spirit that had grown up around the pit heads in the 19th century went some way to offset the dirty and dangerous nature of the job. The result was brotherly unity that was outstanding in the British labour movement. Here three pit boys share a joke at the end of a day's work in the Newcastle coalfield.

OPPOSITE bottom: Keeping the wheels of industry turning. Coal was the fuel on which Britain's industrial success was based. In 1880 alone British miners dug more than 150 million tons of it out of the ground. This photograph, taken in 1910, shows miners with full coal trucks waiting to return to the surface at Bargoed mine near Cardiff.

ABOVE: Pit ponies played an important part in the mining industry. They were used both at the pit head and underground, where they pulled coal trucks to and from the workface. These miners are leading their ponies back to work after the settlement of the 1915 coal strike in South Wales.

LEFT: Going up. This famous photograph of the miners' lift at Frog Lane Pit in Bristol in 1905 gives an idea of working conditions in Britain's coalmines at the beginning of the century. These lifts, which look like sardine cans on end, were wire cages winched up and down by cable. Each held a maximum of five miners. Both going underground and returning to the surface the journey took place in darkness, and there was often a long walk to and from the coalface at the beginning and end of the day.

OPPOSITE: The smoke and chimneys of the northern manufacturing towns were not the whole story of Britain's working life in the late Victorian era. This charming photograph of a woman sitting at a spinning wheel at the door of her cottage shows another side. Spinning was still a part of many housewives' daily working routine in the country, in spite of the great advances in textile technology that had followed the Industrial Revolution.

ABOVE: By the time this photograph was taken at the Shire Show in Islington's Agricultural Hall, the great British cart-horse was already on his way out. They were trotted out for display in agricultural competitions but the internal combustion engine was steadily taking over many of the traditional tasks on the farm, in industry and for transportation. The pride of this fine specimen, however, appears undaunted by the prospect of early retirement.

WOMEN IN THE WORKFORCE

THE first two decades of the 20th century saw one of the most significant changes in the pattern of working life in Britain. Traditionally, the place of the married woman in Britain had been the home. She was responsible for managing the household, with or without the benefit of servants, while her husband was out earning the family's daily bread. For the unmarried woman, the only employment opportunities were in domestic service. Every upper-class and many a middle-class home had its scullery-maids, chambermaids, kitchenmaids and nurserymaids. By the end of the Victorian age one in three women in Great Britain was a domestic servant. As the photographs on this page show, the physical conditions of this upstairs–downstairs world were often very much more comfortable than those of the crowded homes the girls had left. Accommodation and uniforms were provided and there was often a sense of community 'below stairs'. But not all households were stately homes presided over by kindly mistresses. Some servants were undoubtedly overworked and poorly treated. Often they worked long hours for low pay with little hope of escape except through marriage. The increase in commerce during this period created new opportunities and women became typists, shopkeepers and so on. But for those who wanted a professional career, the upper ranks of nursing were as high as most women could expect to go.

Suddenly, with the outbreak of the First World War, all that changed. The tide of young men that flowed to the recruiting offices and from there to the Western Front left many essential jobs vacant back in Britain, and women were quick to fill them. Whether as factory hands (*opposite top and middle*), bus conductresses or chimney sweeps, they proved themselves more than equal to men. Women also did some of the most dangerous home-front jobs of the war, such as working in munitions factories (*opposite bottom*). Indeed, without them the war effort could hardly have continued.

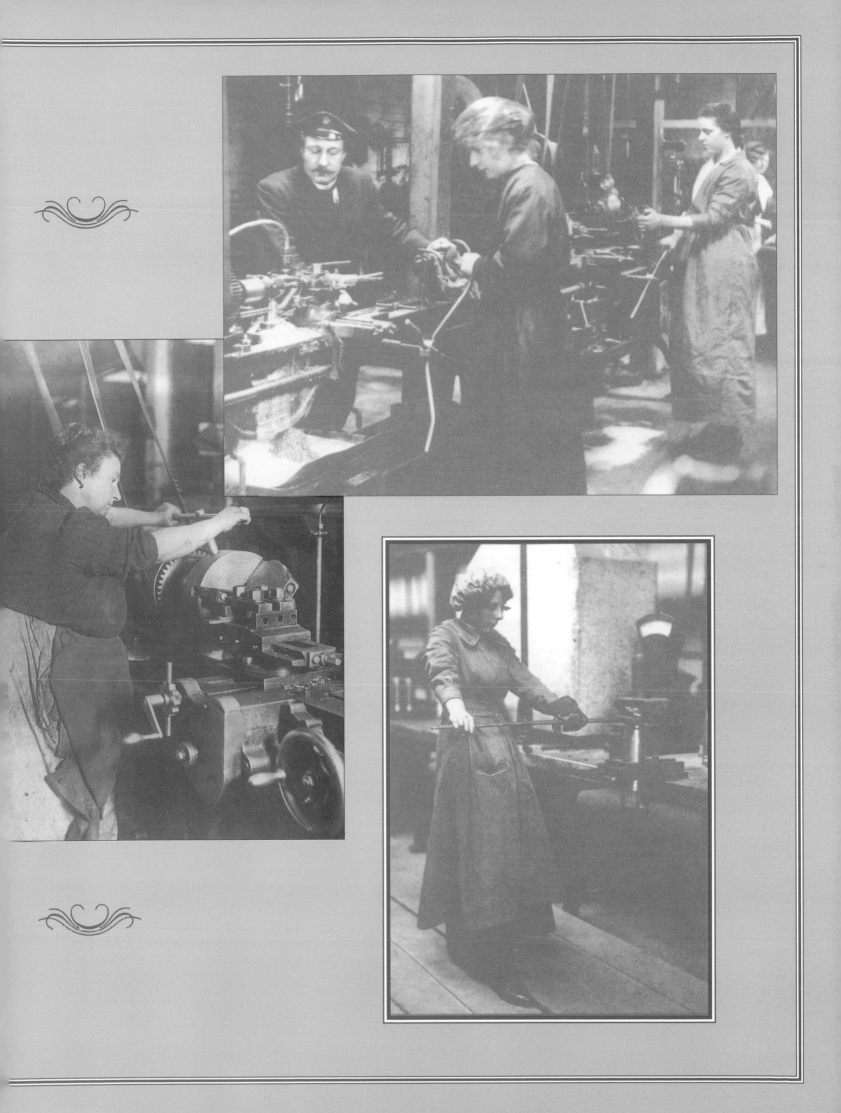

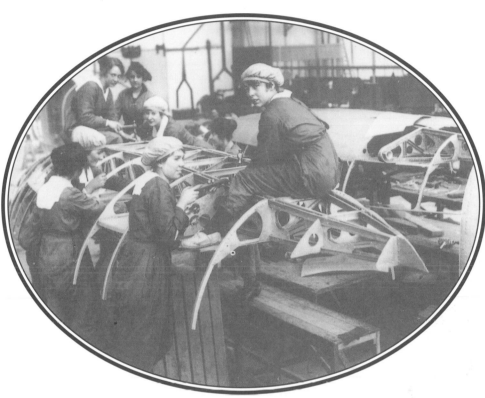

THE transport revolutions of the 19th and early 20th centuries made sweeping changes in the working life of the country. They also opened up more job opportunities. *Left*: How many men does it take to build a locomotive? Workmen with one of the products of their handiwork at the Great Western Railway works in Swindon, 1875. *Above*: Up, up and away. Women workers building the frame of an airship gondola at Short Brothers in February 1919. Many would lose their jobs when all the troops had returned from the front.

FOR many workers, just like today, the canteen was an important social centre, especially as it was where the day's gossip was exchanged. No doubt one of the subjects on the lips of these bus drivers and conductors in the canteen of the Euston Bus Garage in London was the coming of the motor bus and the passing of its horse-drawn predecessor. That was a recent development when this photograph was taken in May 1911.

WHAT the canteen was to the midday break, the pub was to the evening. It is easy to guess the main subject of conversation of these Welsh coalminers enjoying their pints in February 1912. That very month the Miners' Federation had begun a national strike for better pay. The call was for 'five and two' – a minimum wage of five shillings (25p) per shift for men and two shillings (10p) per shift for boys.

FAR removed from the grime and danger of the miners' shifts in the collieries of South Wales was the working life of this well-turned-out young man. Employed by a commercial undertaking in the City, he would spend his days in an office. Off-duty here, he stands proudly outside the neat fence of the brick-built home in suburbia to which he returns at the end of each day.

A small yet significant victory was gained in the struggle for better working conditions in 1888. A handful of female workers at Bryant & May's match-making factory in East London *(right)* struck for better pay. One of the main forces behind the industrial action was Annie Besant *(left)*, a campaigner for women's rights. She was appalled by the dangerous conditions in which the match-girls were expected to work and the pitifully low wages they earned. She helped them to organise the strike and used her weekly journal *Link* to publicise their cause, which was also taken up by others. The successful outcome of the strike was seen as a sign that unskilled workers could gain improvements in their working lives by organising themselves. It was an important step on the road to the 'new trade unionism' of the closing years of the century.

WAR YEARS

O N 28 June 1914 a shot rang out on the streets of the Bosnian capital, Sarajevo, that was to echo throughout Europe for the next four years and change the face of British life for ever. The assassination of the Archduke Franz Ferdinand and his wife by a Serbian gunman was the first of a chain of events that led to war between Britain, France and Russia on the one hand and Germany and its allies on the other.

The immediate cause of Britain's entry into what was to become the tragedy of the First World War was the German invasion of Belgium, a neutral country which Britain had promised to defend. The decision to go to war was greeted with a wave of patriotic fervour throughout the country. Young men flocked to the recruiting offices in multitudes and soon after the new soldiers embarked for the continent to confront the power of the German army. Many believed the war would be over by Christmas, but within a few weeks the patriotic dream had become a nightmare. The opposing armies dug themselves into the trenches of the Western Front in a stand-off that was to last for four years and claim the lives of millions.

On the home front too the war brought enormous changes. Men from all social classes and backgrounds left for France and Flanders, and the government diverted the productive power of national industry to the war effort. The result was that for a few years there was firm central control over the country's economic life. Women for a while achieved a new position in society, keeping the nation going by doing the jobs their menfolk had left on going to war.

There were some other major social changes. Among them were an increase in local authority housing and improved health care. Trade union membership almost doubled during the course of the war and the Labour Party emerged as a possible alternative government. As the true horror of the Western Front became clear to those who remained behind, the war itself became less popular. Conscription had to be introduced because the stream of volunteers dried up. By the time the conflict ended in November 1918, British life had been shaken to its very foundations.

───── ❧ ─────

M ARCHING as to war. Some of the hundreds of thousands of volunteers who answered the call to arms in August 1914. More than half a million British men volunteered in the first month of the war alone.

IT was not just in civilian work on the home front that women made a distinctive and valuable contribution to the war effort. Thousands of women played their part overseas, many of them acting as nurses in the field hospitals set up to deal with the appalling casualties of war. The most famous of these was Nurse Edith Cavell, who was popularly viewed as a martyr after she was shot by the Germans on 12 October 1915 for helping British and French prisoners of war to escape in Belgium. In addition, many

adopted military uniform, among them these members of the Women's Signalling Corps seen under inspection in February 1916 *(opposite top)*.

A less formal side of military life is revealed in the photograph of smiling and cheering Waacs (members of the Women's Auxiliary Army Corps) at a military wedding in the last months of the war *(opposite bottom)*. In the midst of hostilities many aspects of life went on much as usual.

ONE of the most important of the new roles played by women in the workforce during the First World War was that of the 'munitions girl' *(above)*. The outbreak of war meant that the munitions industry had to expand rapidly and efficiently to supply armaments for the front. At the same time because of the flood of volunteers to the recruiting offices – more than 2 million in the first 18 months of the war – industry lost many of its traditional workers. It was women like this one who stepped into the breach.

ABOVE: Showing the flag. Children loyally wave their Union Jacks during Empire Day celebrations at their school. The First World War was not just a war for King and country. It was a war to protect the far-flung British Empire as well.

OPPOSITE top: The home front. Schoolboys in London's Hyde Park imitate the actions of their elders by digging themselves in at the beginning of the war. In later years the reality of trench warfare became known, particularly after the catastrophic battles of 1915 and 1916. Only then did the patriotism of the majority of the British people show signs of waning.

OPPOSITE bottom: Children of Britain say 'Go'. Schoolboys playing bagpipes and waving Union Jacks march down Whitehall from Trafalgar Square as part of the government's first big recruiting drive after the outbreak of war in August 1914. Before the end of the war some of them would be old enough to fight themselves.

ON DUTY AND OFF DUTY

WHILE Britain's politicians argued amongst themselves about the best way to conduct the war, the soldiers on the Western Front suffered appalling losses. The action quickly became bogged down. The opposing forces dug themselves into trenches defended by machine guns and barbed wire, confronting each other across a no-man's land of mud and shell-craters *(opposite middle)*. The British 'Tommies' made themselves at home – those shown here *(opposite bottom)* are making puddings. The pattern was set by which the war was to continue for the next four years. Men went 'over the top' in waves, only to be mown down by enemy gunfire. In 1916 Britain lost 60,000 men, of whom 19,000 were killed on the first day of the Battle of the Somme alone.

Matters were equally desperate on the Eastern Front. In 1915, in an attempt to break the stalemate in the West, a huge allied force landed at Gallipoli in the Dardanelles. It suffered tremendous losses at the hands of the dug-in German and Turkish defenders. This action involved large numbers of New Zealand and Australian forces *(seen, opposite top, with their kangaroo mascot)*. It was partly devised by Winston Churchill, then First Lord of the Admiralty, and David Lloyd George, then Minister of Munitions, here seen together in London *(left)*. Churchill's reputation was severely dented and he was soon demoted. Lloyd George, on the other hand, became head of the wartime coalition government in 1916.

BELOW: Military aircraft, used for the first time during the war, had been tested as early as 1912. Here soldiers try to keep a plane steady as the propeller is started up, with undignified results!

WOMEN had been campaigning for the right to vote for many years. The government tried firm counter-measures, such as the so-called Cat and Mouse Act and the force-feeding of suffragist hunger-strikers in prison. Marches such as this one by the Women's Political and Social Union in 1911 *(right)* kept the issue high in the public mind. Only weeks before war was declared, one of the leading lights of the movement, Mrs Emmeline Pankhurst, had been arrested outside Buckingham Palace; she and her fellow-campaigners had tried to present a petition to King George V *(above)*. However, many suffragists supported the action against Germany, and once war was declared even Mrs Pankhurst took an active part in the government's recruitment drive. The high-profile role of women during the war years persuaded the government that they should be given the vote. In the Representation of the People Act of 1918 the franchise was at last extended to women. Those over 30 who were ratepayers or married to ratepayers were eligible.

RIGHT: In the early stages of the war the government hardly needed its recruitment campaigns to persuade people to sign up for the army. Hundreds of thousands of men wanted to volunteer and only needed to be told how to do so. However, the recruitment drive was a vigorous and varied one, including lively notices on pillar boxes and the famous poster of Lord Kitchener, Secretary for War, pointing towards the reader above the words 'wants YOU'.

BELOW: London's Trafalgar Square, the site of a monument to Nelson, hero of an earlier war, became the place for regular public meetings between 1914 and 1918. It was used both in support of the war and, more rarely, in opposition to it. The message carried by these street boys, parading in makeshift uniforms in front of one of the government's huge recruitment posters shortly after the outbreak of war, is clear for all to see. A game for them, war was already inescapable reality for thousands in France and in Flanders.

ABOVE: Trafalgar Square again, with a crowd shown listening closely to a rousing speech by one of the many women who played an active part in the government's recruitment drives. One of the most famous recruitment posters of the war featured a mother, her daughter and a young curly-haired child standing at the window of their house while the end of a column of uniformed men marched off into the distance outside. The message read simply: 'WOMEN OF BRITAIN SAY – "GO!"'.

ABOVE: War fever affected every class of society in Britain. In this curious photograph, taken in 1916, soldiers are seen driving through London's Hyde Park with lady flag-sellers. Despite the enormous changes that were taking place in society, members of the upper classes – such as the rather chilly-looking family with the pony – still came to Hyde Park to take the air. On still nights the sound of the guns in France could be heard in the distance in London's fashionable drawing rooms.

RIGHT: The returning hero. A soldier arrives at the door of his family home to pick up the threads of his life after four years away at war. Many, though, after the initial joy of reunion, faced unemployment or, at best, a return to low-paid jobs. They had been promised a 'land fit for heroes to live in', but those who survived the mass-destruction of the Western Front returned to find Britain on the edge of economic depression.

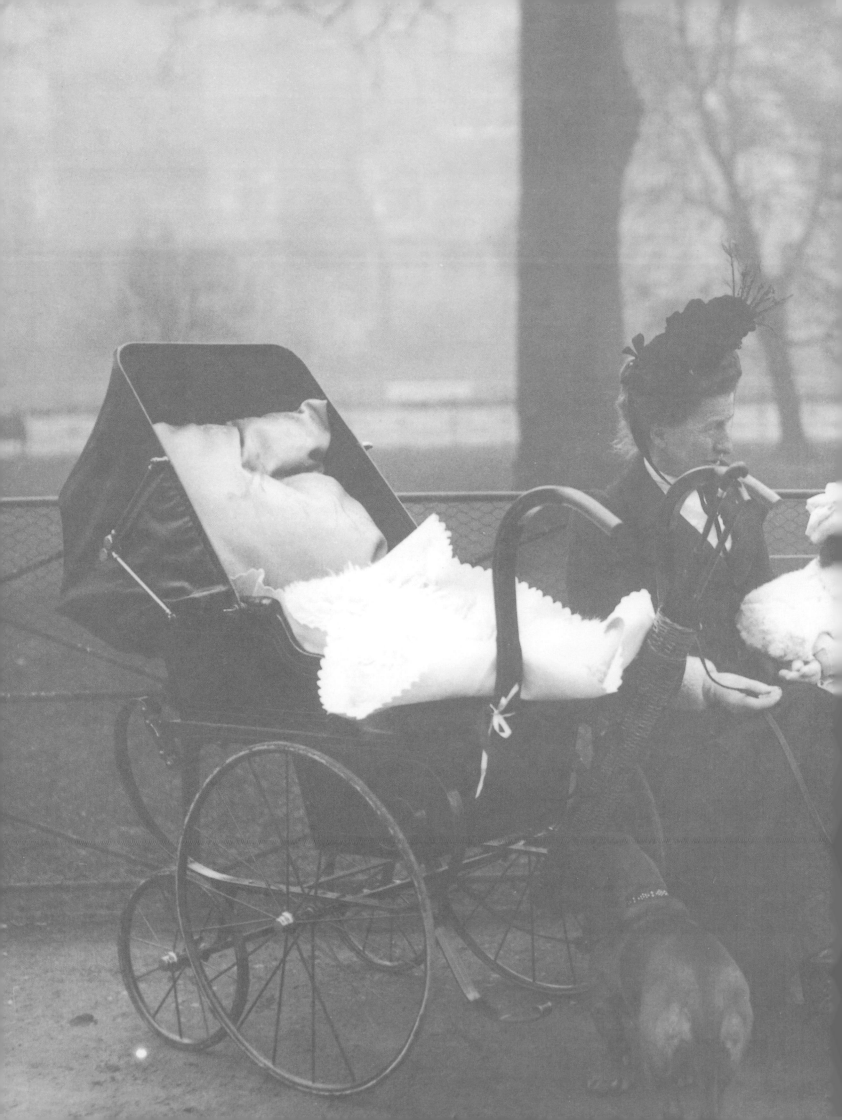

FAMILY LIFE

IF there is one institution above all others that has come to sum up the Victorian era for us today, it is the family. For the Victorians, the family was a miniature of society, an ordered world in which every member had his or her part to play under the firm but kindly eye of an ever-watchful father. Family values were seen as the highest expression of Christianity. Furthermore, they were the moral foundation on which the British Empire was constructed.

These were ideals, of course, and everyday life often fell short of them, especially in the homes of the less well-off. But family life remained at the very centre of the Victorian view of the world and has provided us with some of the most familiar and long-lasting images of the last century, as well as some of the most touching. Given the high ideals which the Victorians held in relation to the family, however, it is perhaps not surprising that there is an air of solemnity in even the most light-hearted of the photographs in this section.

In fact, by the time Queen Victoria's long reign came to an end in 1901, there had already been important changes in the pattern of everyday life. For one thing, there were fewer children grouped around the average family hearth at all levels of society. The usual family size was still much larger than it is today, but it was starting to fall towards modern levels, not only among the most wealthy but also among ordinary working people. Since the working man – there were almost no married women who worked – also found he had more money in his pocket in the last quarter of the 19th century, living standards began to improve too. Some of the familiar routines of today's family life were beginning to appear. There was better and more varied food on the family table, fewer children went out to work at an early age and more and more people found they could afford an annual family holiday. But some of the most significant changes of the 20th century lay ahead. By 1919 there would be hardly a family in the land that was untouched by the tragedy of the Great War.

OTHER people's children. Two well wrapped up young ladies visit the park with their nanny – but why with a pram when there is no baby? The professional nanny was one of the most important figures in Victorian and Edwardian family life, at least in the better-off families.

THE poorest families went short of the basic things they needed. The prosperous families – which were far less numerous – had money for luxuries. Among those luxuries was photography, so there are far more visual records of the rich than there are of the poor. *Above*: A group of children pose with their very Japanese-looking parasols at Richmond Regatta in 1917. *Right*: Miss Kennedy Scott, dressed more for the drawing room than for the gymkhana, reins in her rocking horse in May 1904.

MONARCHS of all they survey. These two babies, pictured in about 1900, had more than most. The eldest, in the pram on the right, is the future King Edward VIII, whose love for the divorcée Mrs Wallis Simpson would throw the country into turmoil and would lead to his abdication in 1936. The baby is his younger brother, whose life would also be turned upside down by the abdication. He succeeded his brother as King George VI, the father of the present Queen.

'THE rich get richer and the poor get children'. Although the size of the average family declined in Britain from about the 1870s onwards, large families were still far more common than they are today. This photograph, taken in June 1914, shows the Terry family of Greenwich in South London. In fact, this is only part of the family – the Terrys had a total of 19 children. It is astonishing that they all grew up in the small terraced house outside which they are pictured here.

A more typical working family is shown here, grouped around the domestic hearth. The two girls, who look as if they might be twins, are helping their mother take care of the youngest member of the family, who is tucked up safely in his crib. It is interesting to note that the boy riding his rocking horse is wearing a skirt and pinafore. It was not at all unusual at this time for boys to wear their older sisters' hand-me-downs for the first few years of life.

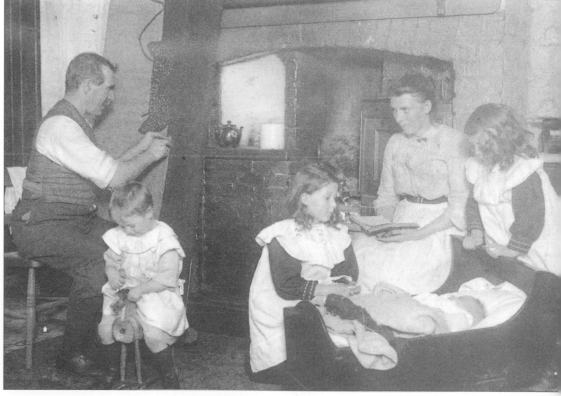

POSED FOR POSTERITY

SOMETHING of the atmosphere of family life in the Victorian home is recaptured in the photographs on these pages. Although the overall impression is one of formality, there was obviously a great deal of fun to be had too. That is being demonstrated *(top right)* by the little boy whirling the tent-like framework for one of his sister's needlework exercises!

Embroidery and needlework were an important part of the routine for girls in Victorian and Edwardian households. In the absence of such labour-saving devices as electric sewing machines and with no mass-produced clothes on the market, hands could not stay idle during an evening's family conversation. Without the ready-made entertainments of television and radio, reading aloud would have been another regular feature of an evening in homes such as the ones pictured here. Singing around the piano or harmonium would have taken the place of the modern hi-fi system on festive occasions. Although there was a marked falling-off in regular church going in the last decades of the 19th century, there were a great many households in which the day still began and ended with the family and servants gathering for prayers.

One of the most striking features of these photographs is that they show just how cluttered the rooms were in a well-to-do 19th-century household. The Victorians had a love of ornaments and bric-à-brac. There is hardly a surface without its porcelain vase, its gilt-framed portrait or its candelabrum. Pets were also an important part of the household, as can be seen from the intricate domed birdcages in the background and foreground of the photographs on the far right, and by the eager interest with which the family on the right are observing their cat's attempts to capture a goldfish!

THE smooth running of the Victorian home depended on a number of routine tasks that are carried out today by the flick of a switch. There were fires to light, coppers to boil for washing laundry and mangles to turn for wringing it out afterwards, to name but a few. In well-to-do homes these tasks would be part of the duties of servants such as this maid, seen delivering a night-cap – complete with lighted candle and a rug for warmth – to her master or mistress. Lower down the social scale, such tasks could take up most of the time of the hard-pressed housewife.

ONE task that hasn't changed in the century or so since this advertisement appeared is that of dusting and polishing, though the brand names have. These were tasks that were performed in most middle- and upper-class households by maids such as the one here seen discovering the miraculous properties of Brooke's soap. Notice the row of bells in the top right-hand corner, which would have rung in the servants' hall 'below stairs' when anything was wanted by the master or mistress in the house above.

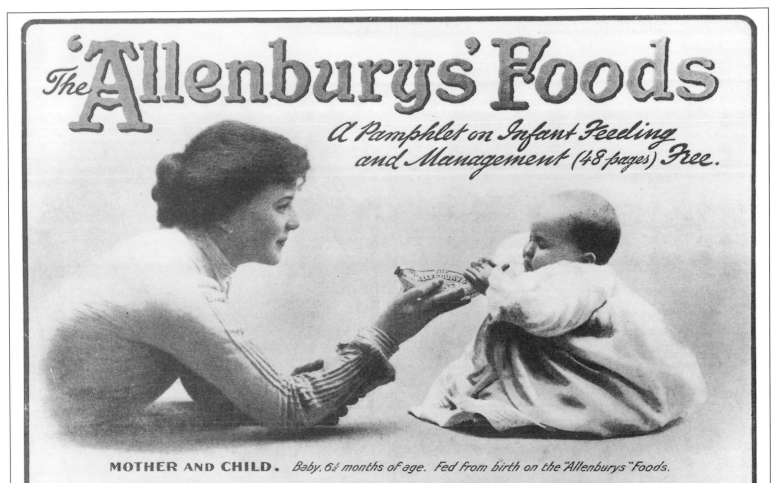

The "Allenburys" Foods give Strength and Stamina, and supply all that is required for the formation of firm flesh and bone. They promote perfect health, and give freedom from digestive troubles and the disorders common to children fed on farinaceous foods, condensed milk, or even cow's milk.

Allen & Hanburys, Ltd., Plough Court, Lombard Street, London.

FOR married women around the turn of the century work more often than not meant managing the household. In the case of the better-off, this was a matter of directing the servants. In the largest houses these would comprise a veritable army of butlers, bootboys, chambermaids *(right)*, kitchenmaids, nurserymaids and so on – it would be a major exercise in itself to manage those. For those who were not able to afford such help, it was a matter of long hours of hard physical work, with few of the labour-saving advantages – from running water to refrigerators – now to be found in almost every home. Not for them either was the luxury of a professional nanny, though one suspects that the immaculately turned-out young woman seen with her baby in the charming advertisement above would probably have handed the task over to one under normal circumstances.

THESE days we think of a typical family as consisting of husband, wife and two children, one of either sex. This is not, in fact, typical even today, but it was still less so in Victorian times. Then, even with the decline in the birth-rate that had taken place during the last twenty or so years of the 19th century, families such as the one here seen posing for the camera outside their house *(above)* would have been the exception rather than the rule. It is interesting to notice that even a household on this modest scale employed two maids.

RIGHT: A phalanx of governesses, nursemaids and their young charges in about 1880. These real-life Mary Poppinses look as if they would have taken very little nonsense from the children who were entrusted to their care.

CHILDHOOD DAYS

THE fall in the birth rate in the last quarter of the 19th century meant that by the the end of Queen Victoria's reign most children were growing up in smaller families than their parents had belonged to. In other words, there were still plenty of uncles and aunts to bring them gifts of money, ribbons and sugared almonds, but not so many brothers and sisters to play with around the home.

What life would have been like for a child of those times depended very much on the social class into which he or she had been born. For the upper classes, childhood would have been very comfortable by the standards of the day. A boy could expect to see as much – or more – of his nanny or governess as of his own parents. He would probably be sent away to boarding school at an early age in order to be prepared for the authority that would one day be expected to fall on his shoulders. A girl would be thoroughly instructed in the principles of managing a household. She would also be taught a number of feminine accomplishments, such as sketching, singing and playing the piano. At the lower end of the social scale, however, life could be hard indeed. Legislation had limited the age at which children could be sent out to work, elementary education had been made free in 1891 and the school-leaving age raised to 12 eight years later. Even so, in a small, cramped house with little money and many small mouths to feed, adding to the household income was often a higher priority than a basic education. Malnutrition among poorer children was still a major problem in many parts of the country, despite the fact that local authorities were providing some 150,000 children with regular meals by the time the First World War broke out in 1914. The many cheerful faces that can be seen in the photographs that follow are a glowing tribute to the resilience of children and evidence of their ability to find amusement in even the most unpromising situations.

~⚬~

SPARE the rod. In an early instance of student unrest, London schoolchildren eye policemen uneasily on a Shoreditch street during their strike action against the use of corporal punishment in schools in September 1911.

THAT childhood was not all fun even for those from the most privileged backgrounds seems to be the message of this photograph *(left)*, showing two Eton schoolboys posing for the camera in their boaters and starched collars. The English public school system set great store by discipline and the system in the schools often gave older boys great power over the lives of younger ones. The long terms away from home could be a painful time in the life of a child.

THIS Victorian brother and sister *(right)* appear far more contented with their lot, although the boy shows some signs of sulkiness about the lesson his older sister is obviously trying to encourage him to learn. The children's clothes are miniature versions of those their parents would have worn, the boy's outfit – and for that matter his carefully curled hairstyle! – being even more elaborately finished than his sister's.

THE sand pit was a popular feature of children's playgrounds even in the Edwardian period, as can be seen from this photograph, taken in Fulham in London in 1910 *(left)*. A sign of the growing popularity of Britain's coastal resorts for the annual family holiday, this one was described as an 'artificial seaside' and certainly seems to stretch further than many a beach at high tide. The children's clothes may look oddly formal for such games, but were in fact exactly the sort that would have been worn on a real beach at this time.

FUN AND GAMES

THE adult world may have changed a great deal in the hundred or so years since these photographs were taken, but most of the games children can be seen playing here are still just as popular today.

There is something particularly touching about the scene of slum children using a lamppost as a maypole in 1902 *(above top)*. One wonders how many of these street urchins had ever seen a real maypole in its traditional setting of the village green. (It is also interesting to note, from the fence on the right of the picture, that graffiti is not just a modern problem.)

The children of the 1890s *(above)* seem to have found just as much pleasure in looking at the world upside down as their descendants a hundred or so years later do. A game of marbles such as the one played outside the cottage door *(opposite top)* is also still in favour. Football, which had become the most popular male spectator sport by the 1880s, provided hours of entertainment for boys such as these pictured kicking a ball around on a patch of wasteland in Newcastle in the early years of the 20th

century. And just as technology continues to develop, so children's fascination with the latest mechanical gadgetry continues. This photograph of three would-be motorists in 1908 *(bottom right)* captured something of their excitement about the newest form of road transport. Their motor is made of pram wheels, wire and pieces of wood.

WITH no form of universal welfare provision, the lot of children born into poor families could be a desperate one in Victorian and Edwardian times. Various pieces of legislation on working conditions, education and health had done something to improve matters since the first half of the 19th century. However, as the pictures on this page show, poverty – and the grim living conditions linked with it – was still all too common an experience for many children in the slums of Britain's major cities. The three barefooted street urchins pressing their noses against the glass of this London shop in the summer of 1910 *(above)* could never have hoped to afford even the cheapest of its wares. The eager rush of children to the baker's cart in this East End street a couple of years later *(right)* reveals the extent of the deep distress that could be caused even by temporary periods of unemployment or strike action.

BY the early years of the 20th century it was compulsory for all children to attend school between the ages of 5 and 12.

ABOVE: The syllabus of many schools included nature study, which was an important subject for town children who might have little opportunity to experience the workings of the seasonal cycle at first hand. These girls being tutored in the ways of root vegetables look somewhat suspicious of the examples on the desks in front of them!

OPPOSITE top: 'Let us now praise famous men'. The boys and girls of Hugh Middleton School assemble to hear their headmaster pay tribute to the achievements of Captain Robert Falcon Scott, whose death during an expedition to the South Pole had been announced a few weeks before this picture was taken in February 1913. Scott and his companions had died on their way back to base after reaching the Pole, and their determination and self-sacrifice earned them an immediate and enduring place in the list of British heroes.

OPPOSITE bottom: Schools aimed to train the bodies as well as the minds of their pupils, and 'physical education' classes, known universally as 'PE', were part of the syllabus. Here a class of young ladies are put through their paces in a 'Swedish Physical Drill Competition', which involved a combination of dancing and physical exercises. Judging by the expressions that can be seen on some of the faces, the strain was already beginning to tell!

THE worst abuses of child labour were over by the latter part of the 19th century. Legislation had progressively raised the minimum age at which children could be employed. Even in the first two decades of the 20th century, however, most children left school at 12 and went out to work, sometimes in such dangerous industries as coalmining. *Above:* Boys employed in the mines at Wigan bring their brothers to read a notice about strike action in 1912.

THE coal strike of February 1912 won improved conditions for miners, including the setting of a minimum wage for children at the far from princely rate of two shillings (10p) per shift. While it lasted, though, it caused enormous hardship in coalmining communities. Here *(right)* a group of coalminers' children proudly parade the sacks they have filled with odd pieces of coal for the family fire by scavenging on the local spoil heaps.

BESIDE THE SEASIDE

FOR most working people in the 19th century travelling was a difficult and costly business, and was associated with the quest not for pleasure but for employment. By the end of the Victorian era, however, rising standards of living meant that more people found themselves with more money in their pockets and with more leisure time in which to spend it. Travel ceased to be a necessary occasional evil, and for the first time came within the reach of the wage-earner seeking relaxation and fun. The most popular destination was the coast. That great British institution, the annual family holiday at the seaside, had been born.

In earlier times visits to the seaside were something you might have been recommended to make by your doctor. Sea breezes and salt water were regarded as a great tonic, albeit one that could be afforded only by the well-to-do. By the beginning of the Edwardian age, however, an entire industry had grown up to cater for the recreational needs of the working people who flocked to the coastal resort towns for their yearly break. Different resorts developed different characters according to the areas from which they drew their holidaymakers. In the South of England, for example, Southend on the Essex coast and Margate in Kent tended to cater for Londoners from 'working-class' and 'middle-class' districts respectively. The same distinction applied to the entertainments offered by, for example, Blackpool and Southport in the North.

Holiday life in all these resorts was centred on the beach. During the day there were bathing or paddling at the water's edge, donkey rides on the sands, Punch and Judy shows for the children and boat trips for the more adventurous. In the evening there were the pleasures of the pier or the bandstand or of simply strolling along the promenade, seeing and being seen by the other holidaymakers. As the photographs in this chapter show, the seaside was still, by modern standards, a formal and buttoned-up place. As a haven from the drudgery of so much of daily life, however, the beach provided not only sea, sand and (occasionally) sun, but also a rare escape into sheer indulgence.

'Oh, I do like to be beside the seaside'. Holidaymakers flock to see a popular entertainer doing her song-and-dance routine in the seafront bandstand at Yarmouth in the summer of 1891.

ALTHOUGH there were still one or two places where men were permitted – at certain strictly controlled times of day – to enter the water with nothing on, the usual practice in Victorian and Edwardian times was for men to wear bathing costumes that were almost as all-encompassing as those of their womenfolk. Here three slightly bedraggled-looking bathers shiver for the camera on the front at Broadstairs in Kent.

THESE two lady bathers, photographed enjoying a paddle around the turn of the century, are being far more daring than they would have allowed themselves to be on a more populated stretch of coast. The formality of their dress was typical of Victorian and Edwardian beachwear even at the height of the summer season, as is the elaborate sun hat of the girl farthest from the camera. Less typical is the amount of thigh these young ladies are showing – just the sort of thing to confirm the worst fears of those straight-laced Victorian commentators who saw the trend towards seaside holidaymaking as a descent into moral anarchy!

THE bathing machine was one of the most familiar sights at the British seaside at the end of the last century and the beginning of this one. These cumbersome devices provided an opportunity for bathers – and particularly lady bathers – to change into their costumes in privacy. The machines would then be wheeled down to the water, enabling their occupants to step straight into the waves safe from prying eyes. Perhaps because by the time this photograph was taken the bathing machine had already become something of a curiosity, these two young ladies seem not quite to have got the idea!

STYLED FOR THE BEACH

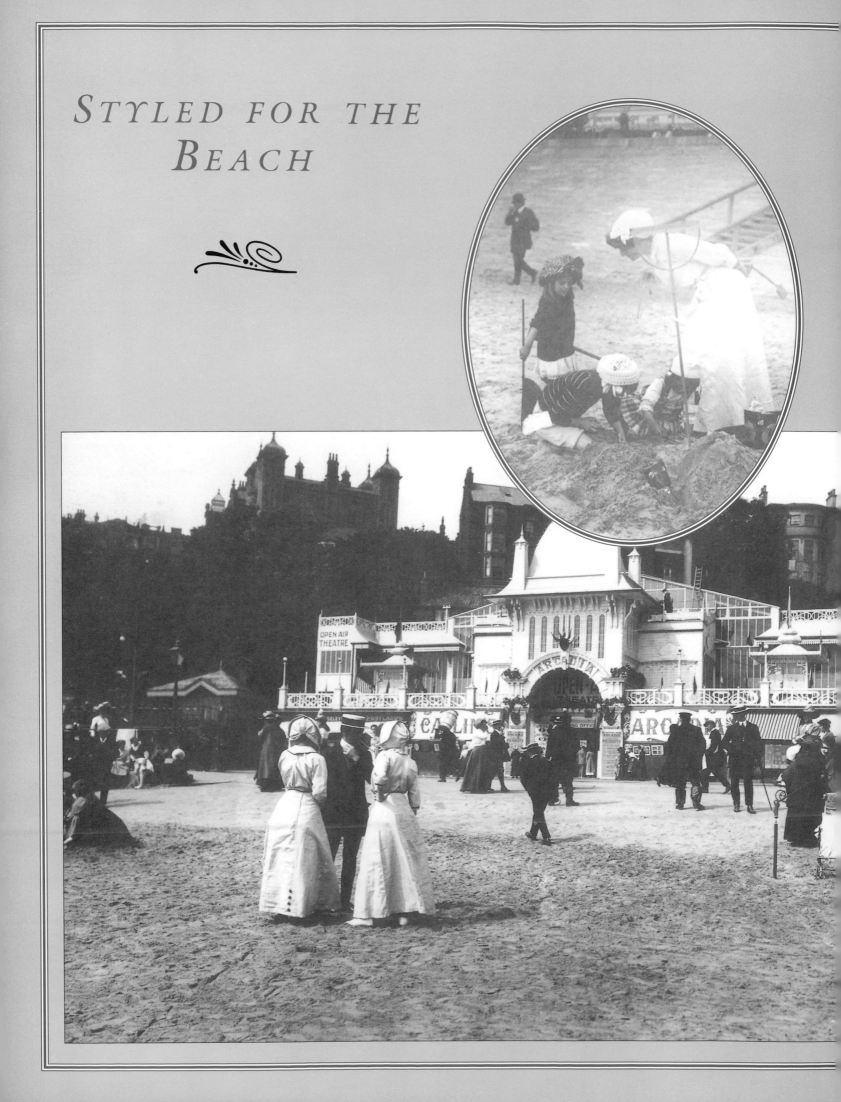

As can be seen from the photographs on these pages, the basic ingredients of beach life have not changed very much in the last hundred years. Even the weather seems to have been as unreliable a factor in the seaside summer holiday then as it is today. The 'brollies' carried by the two ladies in the picture here *(top)* are definitely umbrellas, not parasols to keep off the sun! Only the clothes of these Victorian and Edwardian holidaymakers set them apart from their modern counterparts. Apart from the party of young revellers above, whose striped jacket and 'flapper' dresses seem to anticipate the fashions of the 1920s, the holiday wear of most of these seaside visitors, with their full-length dresses and formal suits and ties, seems more appropriate to a winter drawing room than to the beach in summer.

The activities shown here reveal the eternal fascination of the beach, especially for children. The sandcastle-builders with their buckets, spade and miniature flag and their fishing net for rockpooling could belong to any age, as could the children playing in the background of the photograph at the top of the page. The garish gothic amusement arcade *(left)* is all too familiar a feature of the seafront scene as well, though when this photograph was taken in 1913 it offered entertainment of a very different style from what is found in such places today. The holidaymakers who ventured inside would have found not slot machines and video games, but an open air theatre and the pierrots advertised on posters either side of the gateway.

EVER popular with town children, donkey rides on the sands were a feature of beach life in resorts all over the country, as can be seen from these two photographs, one taken at Blackpool in 1903 *(above)* and the other at Ramsgate two years later.

BLACKPOOL was a popular, and very typical, British seaside resort of the turn of the century. A village at the beginning of Victoria's reign, it grew into a major holiday town after the 1870s. The Blackpool Tower, with its echoes of the recently completed Eiffel Tower in Paris, was put up in 1893 at one end of the broad promenade that became known as the Golden Mile. In the 1880s the Golden Mile saw the first electric trams to run anywhere in Britain. Catering particularly for holidaymakers from the Manchester area, Blackpool was – as it remains – famous for its seasonal entertainments and its funfair.

THE broad sands and towering cliffs of Scarborough on the Yorkshire coast appealed to a more sedate breed of holidaymaker than was attracted to the pleasure beach at Blackpool. One of the first resorts to develop in the mid-Victorian period, Scarborough could boast not only the attractions of a sheltered beach, a picturesque fishing harbour and a ruined castle, but also had the added advantage of mineral water springs. The famous Grand Hotel, seen at the far left of this 1911 photograph, was one of the great monuments of Victorian seaside life and still dominates the seafront today. It is interesting to note that it is built on the site of the house in which Anne Brontë died of tuberculosis – a fact certainly not advertised by Victorian hoteliers seeking to promote Scarborough as a healthful spa as well as a seaside resort!

TAKING IT EASY

FOR the majority of working people in Victorian and Edwardian Britain leisure was a commodity in very short supply. Working hours were long and exhausting and pay too low to cover much more than the essentials of life. But things were beginning to change. The Bank Holiday Act of 1871 added six days a year to the average worker's stock of free time – which gave the opportunity for an excursion to the countryside by train or charabanc, or perhaps to go on a bicycling expedition. Also, an annual holiday by the sea was becoming a regular part of the working calendar for an increasing number of people by the end of the 19th century.

Perhaps the greatest difference from what happens today is that entertainment was very much a do-it-yourself affair. Nowadays the average family spends many hours after work in the evening watching the television or listening to the radio. At the turn of the century such ready-made sources of entertainment were still in the future, and most amusements were home grown. At family gatherings there might be parlour games such as charades to be played, or the family members might group themselves around the piano or the harmonium to sing some of the popular songs of the day. Special occasions might be marked by a visit to the music hall or, during the summer holiday, to the pierrot show at the end of the pier.

As for outdoor entertainments, rambling and – once the price of bicycles came within reach of the average household budget – cycling were popular pastimes, as was boating in the Lake District. The better-off could take to the water on the fashionable stretches of the Thames. In winter skating on frozen lakes or rivers was a frequent source of fun for young and old alike. For those at the top of the social scale, hunting and shooting remained an important part of the social calendar, as did visits to the races. The more sedate, on the other hand, might prefer a game of croquet. It was a fashionable, and often highly competitive, entertainment among the well-to-do.

TALLY-HO: Members of the Pytchly Hunt and the Grand Military Hunt enjoy a luncheon party during a point-to-point meeting in March 1912.

AS this photograph shows *(above)*, it was not only at the seaside that the Punch and Judy show, with its well-known puppet characters and knock-about humour, was a popular form of entertainment – nor was its appeal limited to the younger members of the family. Here adults outnumber children in the audience for a performance on a street corner in Edwardian London.

THEATRE and music hall provided a welcome break from worries about the safety of husbands, brothers and sons serving in the trenches of the Western Front during the dark days of the First World War. *Opposite top*: Wartime pleasure-seekers queue for admission outside the Aldwych Theatre in London's West End.

IN 1901 the Italian physicist Marconi successfully sent the first ever transatlantic wireless message, from Cornwall to Newfoundland, thus ushering in a new era of communications. However, the wireless remained a curiosity for most people until well after the First World War. *Opposite bottom*: Radio days. Four race-goers enjoy the rare pleasure of listening to the wireless in a special saloon on the Grand National train.

DESPITE the disapproval of more puritanical people, who were shocked by the often bawdy humour of such entertainers as Marie Lloyd, visits to the music hall were one of the most popular leisure pursuits for working people in the early years of the 20th century. *Above left*: Black-and-white minstrels such as this one, photographed in 1884, were popular in the days before immigration from Britain's former colonies made race relations a sensitive issue. *Above right*: The famous entertainer Dan Leno as Mother Goose in pantomime.

THE pierrot *(right)* was an essential character in the repertory of seaside entertainment at the turn of the century. Just as the Butlin's 'red-coats' became a training ground for a later generation of popular entertainers, so the pierrot troupes provided a springboard for the careers of such well-known comedians as Max Miller and Stanley Holloway.

THE operettas of W. S. Gilbert and Arthur Sullivan were immensely popular in the late Victorian period and have remained theatrical favourites to this day. *Opposite right*: A scene from an 1880s production of Gilbert and Sullivan's *Patience*, which, for all its fun, was also in its day a satire on the affectations of such end-of-the-century literary figures as Oscar Wilde.

THE country-house circuit of the leisured classes was a closed world to the vast majority of the British people in Victorian and Edwardian times. The privileged round of house parties, balls and hunts remained the preserve of the wealthy few. Central to the aristocratic social scene was Queen Victoria's eldest son, known in his Prince of Wales days as 'Bertie', who was to succeed to the throne in 1901 as King Edward VII. The leader of the sophisticated 'Marlborough House set', he pursued a rakish way of life that was the despair of his puritanical mother, but endeared him to many ordinary people. The Prince of Wales is third from the left, wearing a kilt, in this photograph of a house party at Abergeldie in Scotland.

TAKING THE
AIR

THE entertainments offered by the great outdoors appealed to the spirit of adventure that was so much a part of the Victorian view of the world. Such pursuits as mountain climbing and glacier walking, both of which were in vogue during this period, may not have been to the taste of all. For the more cautious there was always the exhilaration of skating in the winter *(above)*. This was a pastime especially popular in the Fens of East Anglia, where the extensive network of shallow watercourses made it possible to skate for miles along frozen cuts and dykes. Less common, but equally exciting as a winter pursuit, was ice-yachting, here seen in progress on a frozen lake in 1918 *(bottom right)*.

The popularity of the Lake District encouraged many people to discover the pleasures of boating for the first time. Those who liked the sight of sails on water but preferred to stay on dry land could make their way to the local municipal boating lake to sail their model boats, as these Edwardian families are doing on their day out together at Kew in 1903 *(above top)*.

The hazards of more fashionable pastimes are illustrated by the photograph of the ditched aeroplane *(top right)*. Not until 1903, when Wilbur and Orville Wright made their pioneering flight at Kittyhawk in North Carolina, did man succeed in launching a 'heavier-than-air machine'. Accidents such as this one ensured that it would be many years before flying became a popular leisure activity in Britain!

6420. RIDING THE DROMEDARY.
ZOOLOGICAL GARDENS.

L.S.&.P.Cº.

IN the days before television the only opportunity most people would have had to see wild animals of the kind that roamed the more distant ouposts of the Empire would have been to make a visit to the zoo. For Londoners and the increasing number of tourists from the provinces who visited London after the Great Exhibition of 1851, this meant a trip to the great zoological gardens in Regent's Park. London Zoo was founded in 1828 and was a great attraction around the turn of the century – though one guidebook of the 1880s mentioned that its smell was so overpowering that it had to be 'judiciously disguised by numerous flowers'. This doesn't seem to have worried the children seen in these photographs, though judging by some of the facial expressions, the pleasures of a ride on the back of such exotic creatures as camels and elephants were somewhat dimmed by the fear of falling off!

IN June 1914 when this photograph was taken Britain was on the brink of war with Germany and its allies. At home, however, the privileged classes pursued their traditional social round, undaunted by the dark clouds already visible on the international horizon. Ascot was – and remains – one of the high points of the social year. Here two race-goers, sporting their badges for the Royal Enclosure, are studiously ignoring the approaches of a gypsy pedlar.

ABOVE: Water music. A group of gentlemen amateur musicians entertain the local children on the beach with banjo and violin. These Edwardian equivalents of today's buskers are remarkably well turned out, but they seem not altogether to have captured the attention of their audience. Certainly the boy on the far right seems to have found their musical skills less impressive than their dress sense!

RIGHT: Sitting on the dock of a bay. Another harbour and another Edwardian group dressed more elaborately than seems appropriate for the occasion. This photograph is a reminder of what a formal business leisure still was for the middle classes in the early years of the 20th century.

PLAYING HARD

IN most of the leisure activities pictured in this section, there is distinctly more leisure than activity. But there was also an energetic side to Victorian and Edwardian Britain at play. Games-playing was not limited to the parlour. The golf course was a popular resort of the well-to-do, such as this Edwardian gentleman practising his swing on the green at George's Hill. Hunting and point-to-point races remained important events in the social calendar of the country gentry, while during the London 'season' they could remind themselves of the brisker pleasures of the field with a gentle canter along 'Rotten Row' *(below)*. This mile-long sandy avenue, which runs through Hyde Park, was traditionally the place to be seen riding or driving if you were a lady or gentleman of fashion. The name itself is a reminder of how socially exclusive it was, 'Rotten Row' being a corruption of 'route du Roi' – the King's road.

Many large houses would have had their own croquet lawn, and while this was normally the preserve of the family, the domestics might also manage to snatch a game from time to time. This 1910 photograph of a maidservant *(right)* shows her squaring up with her mallet to knock the ball through the next hoop.

More energetic still was the latest craze of the 1890s – bicycling. The introduction of the pneumatic-tyred bicycle opened up a new era in the history of personal transport. The new machines were more comfortable and capable of travelling longer distances than the 'bone-shakers' that preceded them. Men and women from all walks of life took to their new pastime with enthusiasm – even though the results, especially for ladies, were often somewhat undignified *(below)*! At the outset the

bicycles themselves were not cheap, but they cost very little to run and within a few years many journeys that would traditionally have been made on horseback or on foot were being made on two wheels instead.

RIGHT: By 1910, when this photograph was taken, the development of indoor skating rinks enabled townsfolk to enjoy one of the traditional pastimes of the country winter.

ONE of the most popular retreats for Londoners around the turn of the century was Hampstead Heath, 800 acres of parkland north of the city that had escaped the intensive development of the 19th-century building boom. Hampstead had been a spa in the 18th century and still retained – as it still retains today – much of its village character. *Left top*: Two little boys buy ice-creams from a barrow on the Heath in 1892.

MANY of the age-old entertainments of the British countryside had already become curiosities by the turn of the century. They were preserved as part of the rural heritage but no longer practised as living traditions. There is certainly very little that is traditional about the top hats, dress shirts and black ties of this troupe of young Morris dancers photographed arriving for a performance by open-topped bus in 1909!

RIGHT: This photograph could have been taken at almost any time during the last 80 years, but in fact it dates from 1910, which places these two boy scouts amongst the first to join the movement. The Boy Scout Movement was set up by the Boer War hero, Robert Baden-Powell, in 1907, with the intention of teaching self-discipline and practical skills to the future guardians of the Empire. But as the smiling face of the boy on the left goes to show, scouting could also simply be great fun.

SPORTING MOMENTS

THERE is no doubt that sport played an important part in the lives of Victorian and Edwardian men and women. Whether it was a matter of kicking a ball around on the backstreets of a northern industrial town or enjoying a leisurely game of croquet on the rectory lawn before dinner, games were one of the main ways in which those who were lucky enough to have free time chose to spend it. Sports were also a significant element in the education offered by the public schools. The emphasis on team games was designed not only to help create 'a healthy mind in a healthy body' but also to foster the spirit of competition, co-operation and fair play on which the Victorian idea of public life was based.

Spectator sports were also coming into their own as a form of entertainment during this period. Football had been played according to various sets of rules for centuries, but it was only in the 19th century that it took the form in which we know it today. It was during this time too that it became a largely professional activity. The first football club was set up in Sheffield in the 1850s and by the end of the century almost every major industrial town had its own club, as well as its band of keen supporters, who would sometimes take advantage of the improved railway network to follow their team to away matches in other parts of the country. National competitions, such as the Cup and the League, which was founded in 1888, added to the popularity of the game, even though the finals were always held in London (and there was of course no television to relay the action to those who could not attend in person). Cricket too became a popular spectator sport, especially after the County Championship was set up in 1873, some of its players – and especially the almost legendary W. G. Grace – becoming cult figures. The great events of the racing calendar were still associated more with the well-to-do than with the average working man, but betting on 'the horses' was a popular pastime at every level of society, offering the hope of a small addition to the pay packet for the less well-off.

FORE! A lady golfer gets herself out of the rough at Portrush in 1911.

FOLLOWING the hounds was one of the most popular of country sports. As much a social as a sporting event, it offered the local gentry not only the exhilaration of the chase but also the opportunity to catch up on the county gossip. *Opposite top*: A meet of the Cottesmore Hunt in Edwardian times.

OPPOSITE bottom: 'It ar'n't that I loves the fox less, but that I loves the 'ound more.' So wrote the man who first called hunting 'the sport of kings', and it seems to be a sentiment shared by the little girl seen here making friends with the pack at a meet of the West Norfolk Foxhounds in November 1913. The dogs look docile enough, but they would soon be demonstrating their killer instincts at the end of the chase. In the background two members of the hunt prepare to follow them.

EVER since racing began at Ascot in 1711, meetings had been associated with royalty and the upper echelons of British society. King Edward VII, an avid race goer whose horses won the Derby and the Grand National as well as the Ascot Gold Cup, kept up the tradition and introduced a new one – the royal drive along the length of the course. The King died of pneumonia in May 1910, and race-goers at the following month's Gold Cup wore black as a mark of respect, earning the meeting the nickname 'Black Ascot' *(above)*.

MOTORING IN STYLE

THE early years of the 20th century saw a transport revolution that was to change the face of Britain's roads for ever. At the end of the 19th century the motor car was virtually unknown in Britain. It was a luxury affordable only by the rich. Motoring was subject to legislation intended to limit the speed of steam traction engines and individual motor cars were often designed by principles relating more to the horse than to the internal combustion engine.

By 1903, however, all that was beginning to change. In America, the 40-year-old Henry Ford clubbed together with some Detroit business acquaintances to start the Ford Motor Company. Their aim was to produce cars for a wider public. Meanwhile, in Britain car ownership, though still minimal by modern standards – there were probably only about 8,000 cars in the entire country – was now common enough for the government to bring in new legislation. The Motor Cars Act increased the speed limit to 20 miles per hour, imposed penalties for dangerous driving and introduced a new licensing system. In 1904 Charles Rolls and Henry Royce went into business together.

By 1913 the number of cars in Britain had soared to 120,000 and motoring had become a popular pastime, though one still limited to the better off, such as the actress pictured here in 1907 (below).

There was also a thriving motor-racing industry *(right)*, fuelled by stiff international competition to set new speed records (a staggering record of 108 miles per hour was achieved in France by 1906).

LEFT: An early motor car negotiates the Cardiff Open Hill Climb, 1907.

TOP: Refuelling at a Brooklands Race Meeting, 1907.

MIDDLE: Contenders for the Isle of Man Tourist Trophy in the same year.

THERE can be few sports so universally associated with one country and its ways as cricket is with England. Eccentric in its rules, apparently leisurely in its progress and regarded with almost religious respect by its devotees, it is as inseparable a part of the English summer now as it was when this timeless photograph was taken during a match between Worcestershire and the Australian Touring Eleven in 1905.

The game had been played in Britain in one form or another since at least the 18th century, but it was with the creation of the County Championship in 1873 that it began to attract the national following it still enjoys today. The championship was originally a competition for just nine counties.

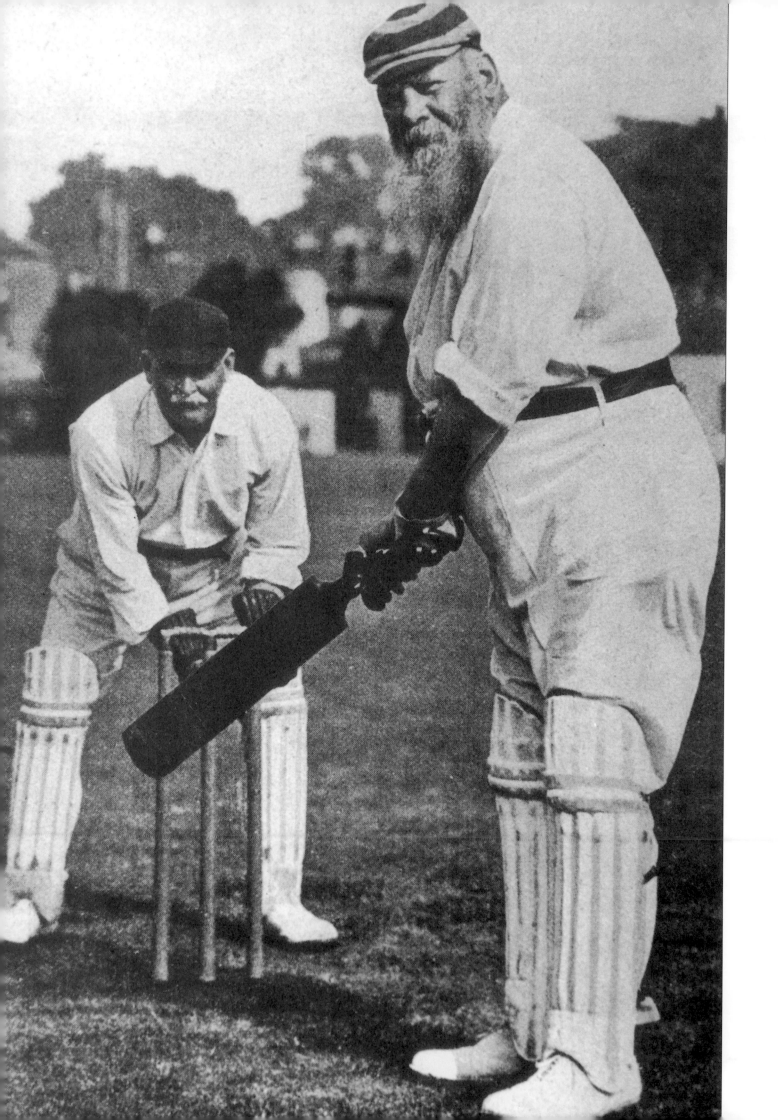

THE man at the crease in this photograph *(left)* was one of the greatest popular heroes of the Victorian and Edwardian sporting scene, Dr W. G. Grace. A Gloucestershire physician, Grace retired from the game in 1908 at the grand old age of 59 after a career that had spanned 43 years and seen him score more than 54,000 runs and take more than 2,800 wickets. A striking figure, with his huge bushy beard and air of natural authority, Grace was often caricatured in his time, but he remained much loved by the British public up to his death in 1915.

MANY of the sports that we might assume to have been exclusively male preserves were in fact as popular with women around the turn of the century as they still are today. One wonders, though, what the autocratic W. G. Grace would have made of this redoubtable-looking cricket eleven (plus twelfth woman) sporting their bats and stumps for a team photograph under a tree in the gardens of Holloway College.

WHILE cricket was popular with a wide cross-section of the British public in Victorian and Edwardian times, shooting was very largely a sport for the gentry and the aristocracy. Indeed, the House of Lords made a point of rising before August 12th – the 'glorious twelfth' – in order that the peers could return to their grouse moors for the start of the annual shooting season. *Above*: Laying out and counting the birds after a pheasant shoot in November 1910.

OPPOSITE bottom: The members of a typical Edwardian shooting party fail to smile for the camera before setting out for their day's sport.

OPPOSITE top: Things seem rather cheerier as the guns break for tobacco and a chat after a good morning's shooting.

ENCOURAGED as character-forming by the public schools of Victorian and Edwardian Britain, boxing was also one of a number of sports in which those from less privileged backgrounds could hope to make a name for themselves. The photograph *(left)* is of Jimmy Wilde, the World Flyweight Champion from 1916 to 1923, who was known as the 'Mighty Atom' on account of his physical strength and diminutive stature.

BY the first decade of the 20th century professional football was attracting a large and devoted following, as can be seen by the size of the crowds lining the stands in the photographs opposite. The action shot *(top)* was taken during a match between Norwich City and Fulham in February 1908. This is an impressive piece of camerawork at a time when exposures could still be long enough to produce multiple images at the slightest movement (see the right hand of the man third from the left in the shooting party at the bottom of page 124). The other one was taken at the beginning of the match between Woolwich Arsenal and Newcastle United that opened the 1919 football season. Unusual when the Football League competition was set up in 1888, it has since become an accepted practice to pay to watch others play.

Once again, the Edwardian woman proves herself anything but the shrinking violet of popular myth. When this advertisement was issued, winter sports were a more exotic pastime than they are today, but there was clearly a market for fashionable ski-wear even then. The message seems to be that the well-dressed woman should ensure she remains well-dressed even when tobogganing!